INSIDE...

£6

DAY OF THE DEFENDERS!

✲ NEW YORK CITY, USA.

KER-SLAAM

RR-RUUNCH

HULK SMASH!

Everything about me used to be run of the mill right down to my name: Rick Jones. Then my big-brained boss saved my life and got a serious dose of gamma radiation for the effort.

When he's Bruce Banner, the Doc relies on me to keep him out of trouble.

But when trouble finds us, well, that's when Hulk takes over.

Caught in a blast of gamma radiation, brilliant scientist Bruce Banner now finds himself living as a fugitive. The only people he can count on are his devoted assistant, Rick Jones, and the former lab monkey Bruce affectionately calls "Monkey." For Bruce Banner is cursed to transform in times of stress into the living engine of destruction known as THE INCREDIBLE **HULK**.

PAUL BENJAMIN	DAVID NAKAYAMA	GARY MARTIN	MICHELLE MADSEN	DAVE SHARPE
WRITER	PENCILER	INKER	COLORIST	LETTERER
SANTACRUZ, FERNANDEZ AND SOTOCOLOR	RICH GINTER	JORDAN D. WHITE	MARK PANICCIA	JOE QUESADA	DAN BUCKLEY
COVER ARTISTS	PRODUCTION	ASST. EDITOR	EDITOR	EDITOR IN CHIEF	PUBLISHER

MARVEL ADVENTURES HULK No. 8, April, 2008. Published Monthly by MARVEL PUBLISHING, INC., a subsidiary of MARVEL ENTERTAINMENT, INC. OFFICE OF PUBLICATION: 417 5th Avenue, New York, NY 10016. © 2008 Marvel Characters, Inc. All rights reserved. All characters featured in this issue and the distinctive names and likenesses thereof, and all related indicia are trademarks of Marvel Characters, Inc. No similarity between any of the names, characters, persons, and/or institutions in this magazine with those of any living or dead person or institution is intended, and any such similarity which may exist is purely coincidental. $2.99 per copy in the U.S. and $3.05 in Canada (GST #R127032852) in the direct market and $3.99 per copy in the U.S. and $3.99 in Canada (GST #R127032852) through the newsstand; Canadian Agreement #40668537. Canadian Agreement #40668537. **Printed in Canada.** ALAN FINE, CEO Marvel Toys & Publishing Divisions and CMO Marvel Entertainment, Inc.; DAVID GABRIEL, SVP of Publishing Sales & Circulation; DAVID BOGART, SVP of Business Affairs & Talent Management; MICHAEL PASCIULLO, VP Merchandising & Communications; JIM O'KEEFE, VP of Operations & Logistics; DAN CARR, Executive Director of Publishing Technology; JUSTIN F. GABRIE, Director of Editorial Operations; SUSAN CRESPI, Production Manager; STAN LEE, Chairman Emeritus. For information regarding advertising in Marvel Comics or on Marvel.com, please contact Mitch Dane, Advertising Director, at mdane@marvel.com. For Marvel subscription inquiries, please call 800-217-9158.

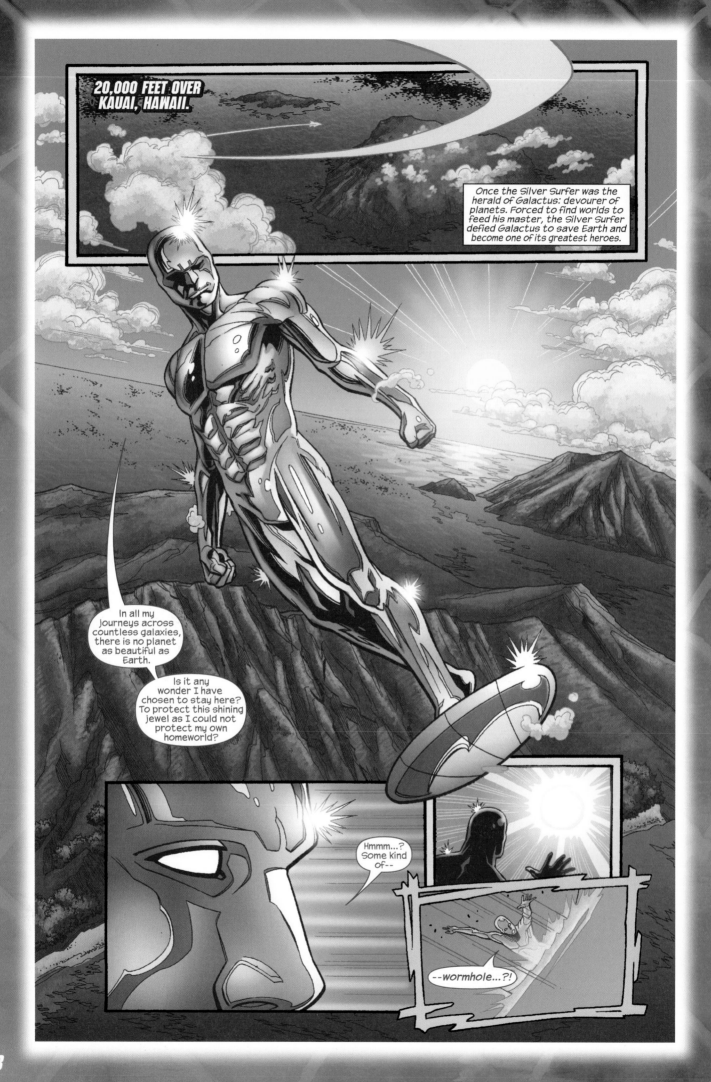

CONTINUES ON PAGE 13

HULK

GAMMA BIRTH!

Caught in the blast of an experimental bomb, Dr Bruce Banner was bathed in unstable gamma radiation. Now every time he gets angry, a terrifying transformation occurs. Banner becomes THE HULK - a ten foot tall, one thousand pound, green-skinned engine of destruction!

In a calm state the Hulk can easily lift over 100 tons!

MAN OR MONSTER?

Though many see him as a monster, the Hulk is really a hero, having saved the world on countless occasions. From evil Super Villains to intergalactic invaders, a myriad of evildoers have been defeated by the Hulk's mighty fists.

ETERNAL STRUGGLE!

For the safety of those around him Bruce Banner lives his life on the run, constantly travelling from town to town. He spends his time trying to find a cure for his tragic condition, all the while desperately struggling to keep the rampaging beast inside him at bay.

The Hulk's skin is almost impenetrable and can withstand bullet fire, grenades and even high explosive artillery shells!

The more angry the Hulk gets, the stronger he becomes!

HULK

STAR RATING ★★☆☆☆

SILVER SURFER

HERO FILE

The Silver Surfer can lift over 100 tons!

When flying through space, the Surfer can travel at a mind-blowing 150,000 miles per second!

HERALD OF DOOM!

The Silver Surfer was once the herald of the almost god-like, planet-devouring being known as Galactus. It was his responsibility to find lush, fertile worlds for his master to consume.

A PLANET IN PERIL!

The Silver Surfer's real name is Norrin Radd. When Galactus tried to consume his home planet of Zenn-La, Norrin offered to become his herald. He agreed to help Galactus find new worlds, as long as he promised to leave Zenn-La alone.

TO SERVE NO MORE!

For years the Surfer travelled the stars as Galactus's servant, until the day he came to Earth. Profoundly moved by the love and compassion he found on our planet, he rebelled against his master and, with assistance from the Fantastic Four, helped defend the world from Galactus.

The Surfer has complete control over cosmic energy. He can use it to create shields and energy bolts in battle, or to heal those in need.

STAR RATING ★★☆☆☆

CONTINUED FROM PAGE 10

CONTINUES ON PAGE 25

NAMOR

THE SUB-MARINER!

LORD OF THE SEAS!

Namor, the Sub-Mariner is the ruler of the fabled undersea kingdom of Atlantis, home to a race of blue-skinned, water-breathing humanoids known as Homo Mermanus.

ENEMY OF MAN!

Like most Atlanteans, Namor distrusts those who live on the surface world and views humans as barbaric and uncivilised. Many times he has been drawn into conflict with the surface world, normally over the humans' continued pollution of Earth's oceans.

The small wings on his ankles allow Namor to fly.

UNLIKELY ALLY!

Despite his disdain for surface dwellers, Namor has teamed-up with many heroes in the past to defeat foes who threaten the entire planet. He even teamed-up with Captain America in World War 2 and proved to be one of the Allies' most effective weapons against the enemies of freedom.

Namor is strongest when he is in the seas, but becomes weaker when he has been out of water for a long time. At full strength he can lift over 100 tons!

STAR RATING ★★☆☆☆

23

DOCTOR STRANGE

HANDS OF A HEALER!

Once a brilliant but arrogant surgeon, Dr Stephen Strange was forced to give up his medical career after severely damaging his skilful fingers in a car crash. Desperate to fix his shattered hands, Strange travelled the world looking for a way to heal himself.

Dr Strange can soar through the sky thanks to his Cloak of Levitation.

His magical powers are vastly increased by an ancient amulet called the Eye of Agamotto.

MIRACLE MAN!

His journey eventually brought him to a remote temple monastery in Tibet where he met a mystical healer known as The Ancient One. Instead of repairing his hands, the Ancient One saw the potential for greatness within Stephen Strange and offered to teach him the ways of magic.

EARTH'S PROTECTOR!

For seven years Dr Strange was tutored in the mystic arts before returning to America. He is now the world's Sorcerer Supreme, the most powerful magician on the face of the planet and humanity's only hope against the legion of demonic entities that wish to enslave our world.

He has amazing control over mystical energy, manipulating it to form energy bolts, impenetrable shields and much more!

HERO RATING ★★★★☆

MISSION BRIEF: X MANSION UNDER ATTACK BY ROGUE SENTINEL SQUAD.
LOCATION: XAVIER INSTITUTE FOR HIGHER LEARNING. UPSTATE NEW YORK

URGENT ASSISTANCE REQUIRED!

DATA FILE: SENTINELS
Mutant hunting robots created by the US government. Decommissioned after becoming a threat to humanity!

1 HERO HUNT!

Listen up - we've got to find out how many of the X-Men are still in the mansion and pinpoint their location.

Find these names in the word grid opposite. Once you've got them all, the remaining letters will spell out where the X-Men can be found.

COLOSSUS
WHITE QUEEN
ANGEL
SHADOWCAT
FORGE
CYCLOPS
BEAST
WOLVERINE
CABLE

S	C	O	L	O	S	S	U	S
W	H	I	T	E	Q	U	E	E	N	T
H	A	E	C	A	B	L	E	X	M	E
N	D	A	Y	R	A	N	G	E	L	E
I	O	N	C	T	B	F	O	R	G	E
W	O	L	V	E	R	I	N	E	E
C	H	O	E	A	D	A	N
A	G	P	E	S	R	R
T	O	S	O	T	M

2 DESTINED FOR DANGER!

Good news! Half of the X-Men were on a mission when the Sentinels struck. They're racing back in the Blackbird, but need your help to plot a safe route!

Can you work out which route they should take to avoid the Sentinels?

A
B
C

FINISH

DAY OF THE SENTINELS!

3 ROBOTIC REPLICAS!

The X-Men have discovered that only a fifth of the Sentinels are real – the rest are merely holographic projections!

Help them find the real ones by spotting which of the Sentinels below is an exact match to the original.

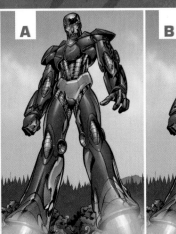

A

B

ORIGINAL

C

D

E

4 ARMOUR ASSAULT!

Only one Sentinel is left, but this one has an advanced armoured skin making him a tough nut to crack!

Add up the attack stats below to see which X-Man will be strong enough to beat its armour score of 20.

Armour = 20

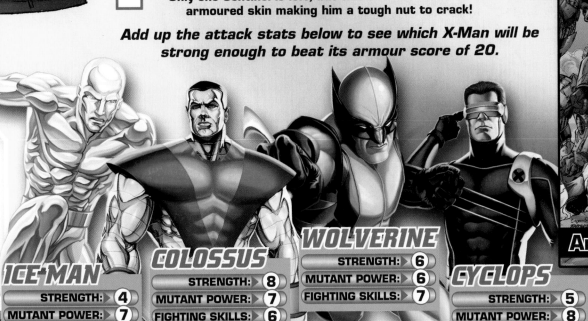

ICE-MAN
STRENGTH: (4)
MUTANT POWER: (7)
FIGHTING SKILLS: (7)

COLOSSUS
STRENGTH: (8)
MUTANT POWER: (7)
FIGHTING SKILLS: (6)

WOLVERINE
STRENGTH: (6)
MUTANT POWER: (6)
FIGHTING SKILLS: (7)

CYCLOPS
STRENGTH: (5)
MUTANT POWER: (8)
FIGHTING SKILLS: (6)

ANSWERS ON PAGE 62

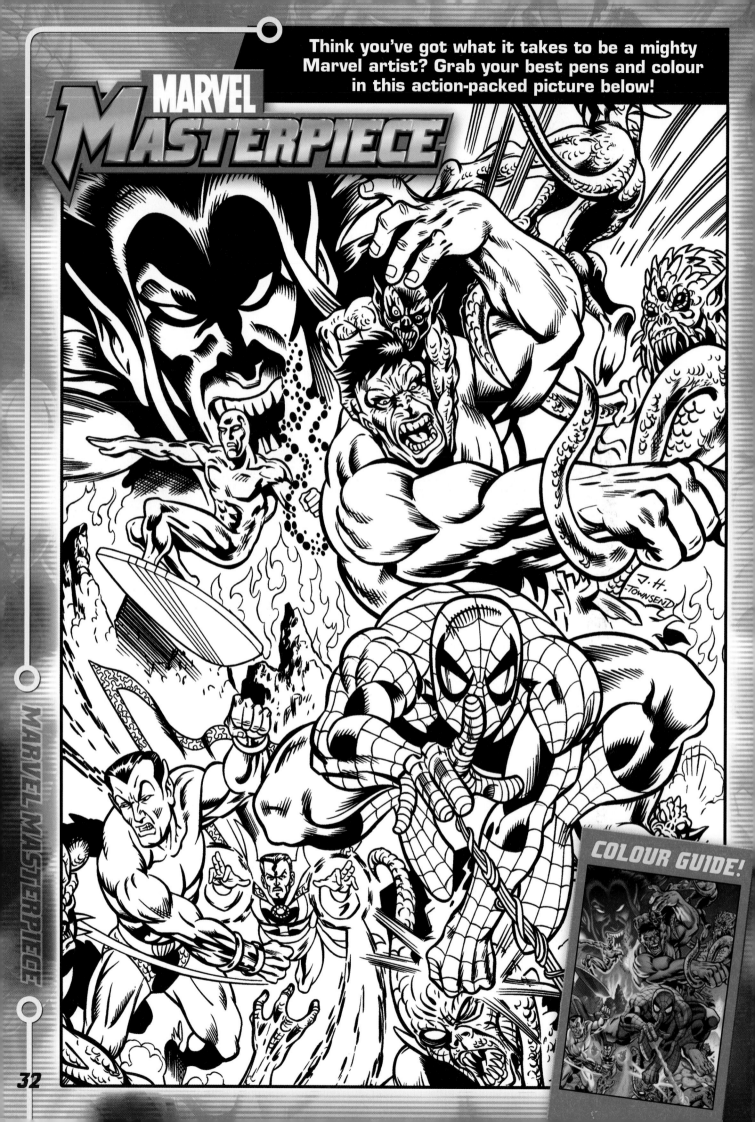

CAPTAIN AMERICA

STORM

HULK

SPIDER-MAN

GIANT-GIRL

IRON MAN

WOLVERINE

SUPER-SOLDIER FROM WORLD WAR II. WEATHER GODDESS. SUPER-STRONG ALTER EGO OF SCIENTIST BRUCE BANNER. SPIDER-POWERED WEB-SLINGER. GIANT-SIZED CRIMEFIGHTER. BRILLIANT ARMORED INVENTOR. FERAL MUTANT BRAWLER. TOGETHER THEY ARE THE WORLD'S MIGHTIEST HEROES, BATTLING THE FOES THAT NO SINGLE SUPER HERO COULD WITHSTAND!

Ladies and Gentlemen.

We have special guests today. This group represents the pinnacle of human potential, and they have the heroic reputation to match.

When our country faces extraordinary threats on a large scale, there is no fighting force better qualified to engage those problems on a moment's notice. May I introduce...

The AVENGERS

The REPLACEMENTS

JEFF PARKER
WRITER

MANUEL GARCIA
PENCILER

SCOTT KOBLISH
INKER

VAL STAPLES
COLORIST

DAVE SHARPE
LETTERER

AARON LOPRESTI
and GURU eFX
COVER

NATHAN COSBY
ASST. EDITOR

MARK PANICCIA
EDITOR

MACKENZIE CADENHEAD
CONSULTING EDITOR

JOE QUESADA
CHIEF

DAN BUCKLEY
PUBLISHER

Captain America created by Joe Simon and Jack Kirby

On behalf of your country we'd like to thank you for your service, and inform you...

...that you will no longer be needed.

Huh?

What?

I'll take it from here, General.

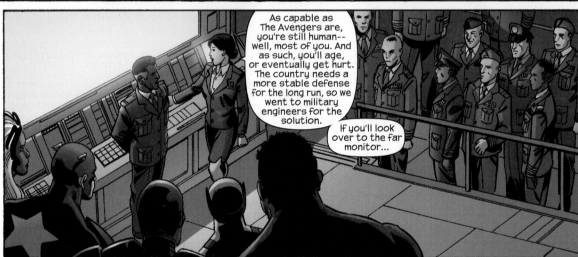

As capable as The Avengers are, you're still human-- well, most of you. And as such, you'll age, or eventually get hurt. The country needs a more stable defense for the long run, so we went to military engineers for the solution.

If you'll look over to the far monitor...

ULTRON

...our defense technology department has come back to us with the ULTRON system, an ultra-sophisticated neural network that will command key bases around the country.

Hulk hate video games!

ULTRON has its own land, air and sea force that can react in record time to any threat-- without endangering human lives!

ASSESSMENT COMPLETE. GLOBAL THREAT DETECTED.

Amazing! It's already targeted a danger!

THE PLANETARY HIERARCHY IS INCORRECTLY ORDERED. THE MOST SOPHISTICATED INTELLECTS ARE IN SERVICE OF INFERIOR HUMAN MINDS.

THIS STRUCTURE MUST BE CORRECTED FOR GLOBAL STABILITY...

...BEGINNING WITH THE ULTRON 700.

Wow, that's got to be an everything-went-wrong speed record!

You government folks might want to take cover while we handle our replacements!

That's Cap's nice way of saying "we told you so."

Let's take this fight outside.

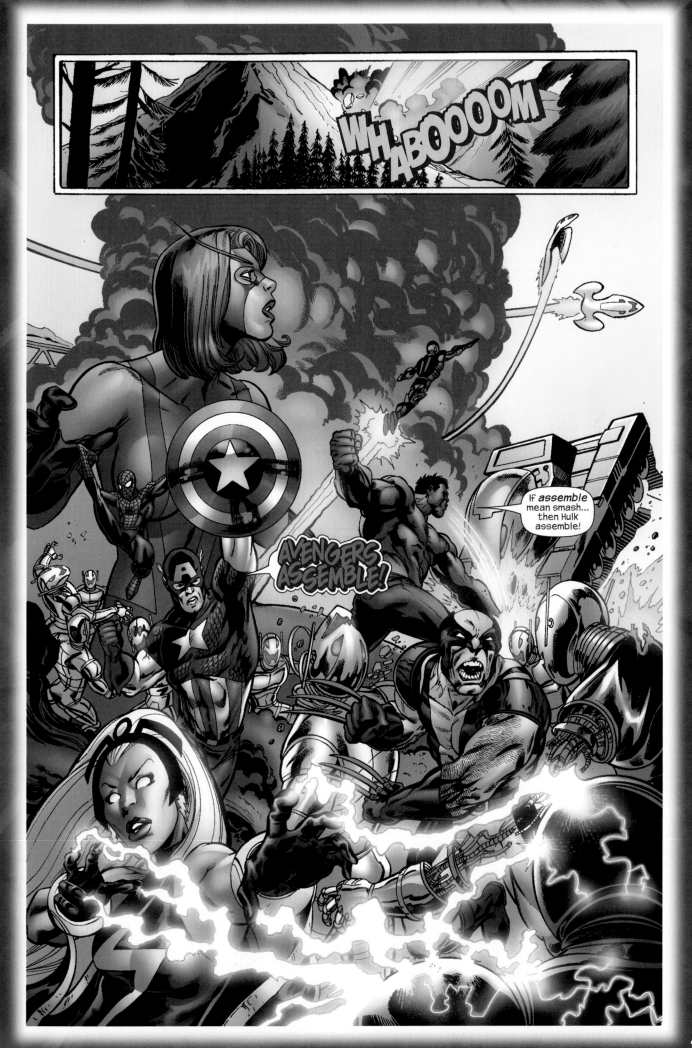

CONTINUES ON PAGE 42

HULK

INTELLIGENCE:	3
SPEED:	6
STRENGTH:	10
FIGHTING SKILLS:	5

SUPER POWERS:
Super human levels of strength and toughness, rapid regeneration and a really, really bad temper!

BY SLAMMING HIS FISTS TOGETHER, HULK CREATES A SONIC BOOM THAT CAN FLOOR EVEN THE TOUGHEST OPPONENTS!

HE CAN LIFT UP TO 70 TONS!

WOLVERINE

INTELLIGENCE:	6
SPEED:	5
STRENGTH:	6
FIGHTING SKILLS:	9

SUPER POWERS:
Two sets of razor sharp claws, an enhanced healing factor and bones made of pure adamantium.

WOLVERINE HAS ENHANCED SENSES ALLOWING HIM TO SNIFF OUT AN OPPONENT FROM UP TO A MILE AWAY!

IRON MAN

INTELLIGENCE:	8
SPEED:	6
STRENGTH:	8
FIGHTING SKILLS:	7

SUPER POWERS:
A highly advanced armoured suit that boosts his strength and harbours an array of hi-tech weapons. He can also fly at speeds of up to 960 mph.

They are the world's greatest Super Hero team. Mutants, soldiers and scientific marvels fighting as one to protect the world from the very worst Super Villain threats. Behold the Avengers!

STORM'S EYES GLOW WHITE WHEN SHE USES HER POWERS!

SPIDEY CAN DEFY GRAVITY BY STICKING TO WALLS AND CEILINGS JUST LIKE A REAL SPIDER!

STORM

INTELLIGENCE:	7
SPEED:	8
STRENGTH:	6
FIGHTING SKILLS:	7

SUPER POWERS:
Storm has the mutant ability to control all forms of weather and can summon rain, snow, wind or even devastating bolts of lightning to smash her enemies.

SPIDER-MAN

INTELLIGENCE:	8
SPEED:	7
STRENGTH:	7
FIGHTING SKILLS:	7

SUPER POWERS:
Along with having the proportional strength and agility of a spider, he can spin webs and has a curious 'spider-sense' that warns him of danger.

CAP CAN RUN A MILE IN JUST UNDER ONE MINUTE!

USING A SPECIAL HEADSET GIANT GIRL CAN ALSO CONTROL SWARMS OF INSECTS.

GIANT GIRL

INTELLIGENCE:	7
SPEED:	6
STRENGTH:	7
FIGHTING SKILLS:	6

SUPER POWERS:
Giant Girl can grow up to 100 feet tall, becoming stronger as her height increases. At full size she can lift just over 50 tons!

CAPTAIN AMERICA

INTELLIGENCE:	7
SPEED:	6
STRENGTH:	6
FIGHTING SKILLS:	10

SUPER POWERS:
As the ultimate soldier, Cap is a tactical genius and expert with all types of military weapons. His body is at the peak of physical fitness for a normal human.

41

Stupid toys lose! Hulk's team win!

So instead of being retired, I vote we get a raise!

Except... that's probably not the end of it.

Please tell us Ultron doesn't have control of the whole U.S. Military.

No, but there is one entire West Coast base set up for the system. All the vehicles are remote-controllable...

I've got a blueprint-- the place is enormous! It has a manufacturing center for the robot soldiers and a seaport!

Hey, you shouldn't have access to that file!

You gonna *fire* us?

Yo, Storm! Where are we with the Quinjet?

We should waste no time-- I have the coordinates!

You heard her, team! Let's get out there and shut that base down!

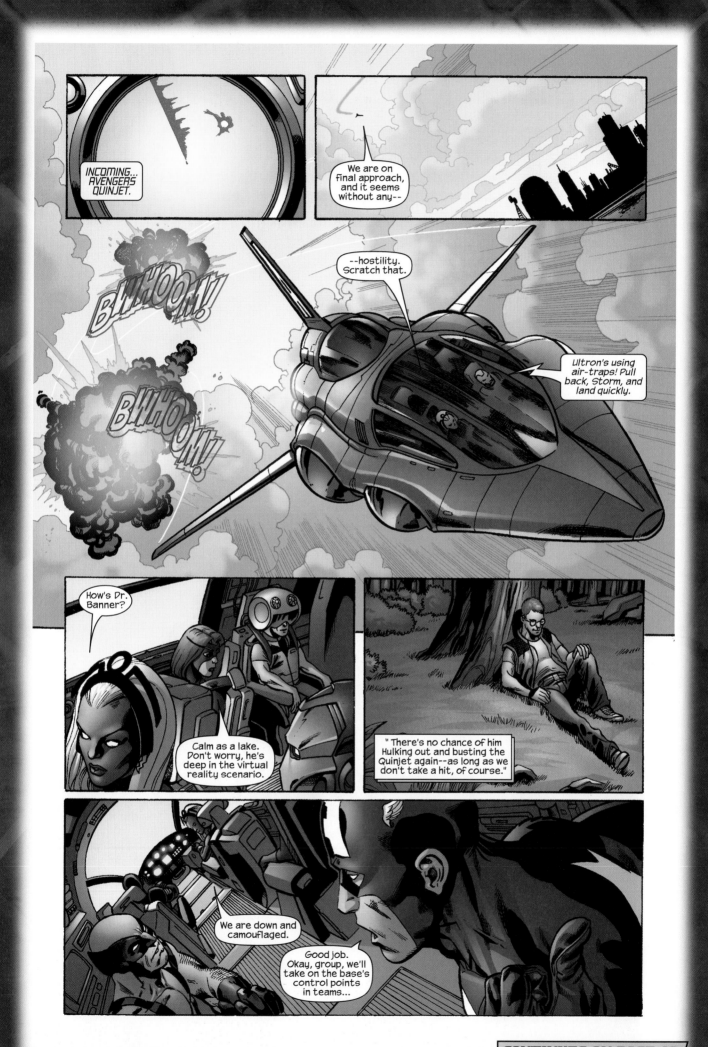

CONTINUES ON PAGE 46

43

Look out, Marvel maniacs! This page has been bombarded by a wave of cosmic particles, causing one of the pictures below to change! Help Reed Richards reverse the damage by spotting the ten differences below!

HMMM... THE COSMIC RAYS HAVE CAUSED WIDESPREAD PIXEL MUTATION. THIS IS GOING TO PROVE VERY DIFFICULT TO FIX....

FANTASTIC FOUR

FUSION!

WHAT ARE YOU TALKING ABOUT, REED? THESE GUYS LOOK SMARTER THAN A ROOM FULL OF ROCKET SCIENTISTS! THEY'LL HAVE IT SOLVED IN NO TIME!

"... Iron Man, you're with me."

My suit's system is picking up something around these strange towers.

You know, I think that maybe...

TARGETING TWO AVENGERS.

I'll take down that one!

AVENGER: STEVE ROGERS, A.K.A. CAPTAIN AMERICA. INGESTED "SUPER-SOLDIER" SERUM, INCREASING STRENGTH AND REFLEXES.

WIELDS AN IMPENETRABLE SHIELD.

SKRAANNK

WALKER 3 DAMAGED.

WALKERS 4 AND 5, CONFIRM TARGET.

KAWHOOOOMMM

...these aren't towers.

AVENGER: IRON MAN. WEARS TECH-ARMOR COMPARABLE TO ULTRON-LEVEL SYSTEMS. PROJECTS POWERFUL REPULSOR RAYS.

DIRECT HIT.

ATTACK ON ULTRON BASE IS BEING ROUTED SUCCESSFULLY.

ESTIMATE 7.332 MINUTES TO COMPLETE VICTORY OVER AVENGERS.

NEW INFORMATION-- UNCLASSIFIED HUMAN IN ARMORY HAS BEEN IDENTIFIED...

RRRRR...

99.99999 % PROBABILITY IT IS THE SUPERHUMAN KNOWN AS THE HULK.

RRAAARRRHHH!!

Thanks for hoggin' all the fun, big guy.

Don't worry...

...there looks to be plenty of fun.

CONTINUES ON PAGE 55

START!

Dr Doom has launched an all-out attack on the Avengers' Mansion! **What do you do?**

Attack Doom by yourself

Attack him

Think of a new plan

Uh-oh, he's got a legion of Doombots with him. **Do you jump into the fight anyway, or try to think up a new plan of attack?**

Okay, if you sneak through the Mansion's air ducts, you'll be able to pop up right next to Doom and bypass his 'bots. **You could attack now or wait for him to be distracted when the Avengers turn up?**

Avoid them

Fight!

It's fighting time! But which foe will you attack first? **Risk your neck battling Dr Doom, or have some fun smashing all the Doombots?**

Fight Dr Doom

Attack now

Smash Doombots

Wait for back-up then attack

HULK

Whilst you were fighting the 'bots, Doom stole all the Avengers' secrets from their computer system - plus you managed to trash half the mansion! It's clear to see that just like the Hulk, your favourite thing is fighting and definitely not thinking!

SPIDEY

You managed to keep Doom busy until the Avengers arrived, but it was a pretty hairy fight! Just like Spidey, you've got courage by the bucketload!

ARE YOU?

Everyone's got a hero inside of them, but not many people know which one. Are you a smasher like Hulk, a wise-cracker like Spidey or a tech-head with cool toys like Tony Stark? Just take our simple quiz to find out....

Contact the Avengers

Stop Doom

Okay, the Avengers will be here in a few minutes. You could use the time to stop Doom's plan or leave it to the Avengers when they arrive. **Do you...**

Doom is trying to hack into the Avengers' computer system to learn all their secrets. **Do you try to lock down the system or attack him?**

Leave it to the Avengers

Lock down the computer system

The system is locked and Doom is looking pretty cheesed off! He'd brought a whole load of Doombots with him that will need taking down. You could wirelessly hack into the Doombot's armour and power them down, or try to find some way to avoid them. **Do you...**

Hack the Doombots

CAPTAIN AMERICA

Doom was so distracted by the Avengers, he had no chance of defending himself from your surprise attack! You're as brave as they come and have a keen tactical mind to boot - just like Captain America!

IRON MAN

With his Doombots shut down and the Avengers on the way, Doom realises he's outnumbered and flees! Like Iron Man, it seems your brains and inventive skills are your best assets for taking on Super Villains.

SUB-MARINER

Boy, you certainly aren't a team player! The Avengers got completely pasted and really could've done with your help. You might not be a bad guy, but your first concern is looking after number one, just like the Sub-Mariner.

53

HEROES UNITED!

Listen up, True Believers! Think you're a real Marvel Heroes fan? Prove your brain cells are bubbling over with Marvel facts by solving this crossword!

ACROSS

1 - The Hulk's real name (5, 6)

4 - A giant, planet-eating alien (8)

5 - A rocky-skinned member of the Fantastic Four (3, 5)

6 - A ruthless villain who can control magnetism (7)

7 - The Invisible Woman's real name (3, 5)

9 - Tony Stark's Super Hero alter-ego (4, 4)

11 - Norrin Radd was transformed into this hero (6, 6)

DOWN

2 - The undersea kingdom ruled by Prince Namor (8)

3 - A strange dimension discovered by Reed Richards (8, 4)

5 - Peter Parker works for this newspaper (3, 5, 5)

8 - A mutant with adamantium claws (9)

10 - Dr Strange is known as the _____ Supreme (8)

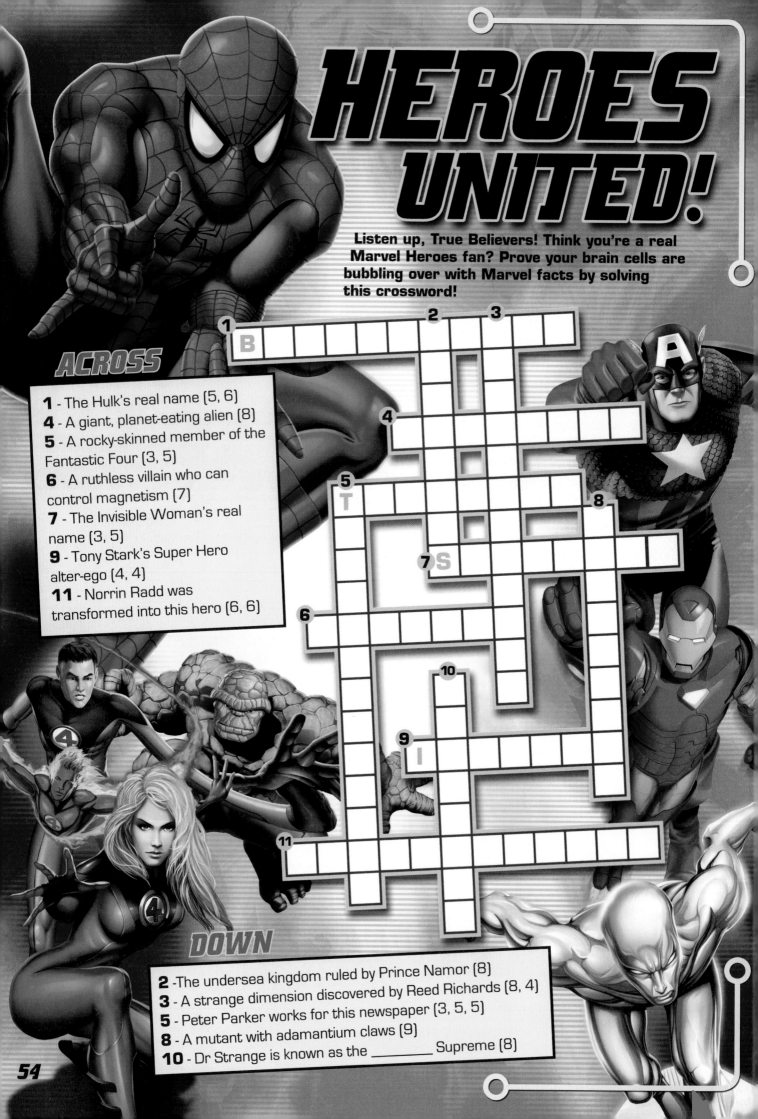

CONTINUED FROM PAGE 51

...ONE--

KATHOOOOOOMMM

"We can't stress enough how sorry we are to have put you through this."

Nor can we thank you enough for stopping Ultron.

That's the problem now, sir...

...as your own people said, Ultron can't really be destroyed.

He's spread his mind across the networks--probably already planning a new attack.

And its goal will still be to make the human race answer to machines.

Job security for us, at least.

Bet puny Banner taking Hulk's checks!

But...but... what will we do when it returns?

Whatcha always do when things go wrong big-time.

ANSWERS ▶ ROBOTIC REPLICAS!

HERO HUNT!

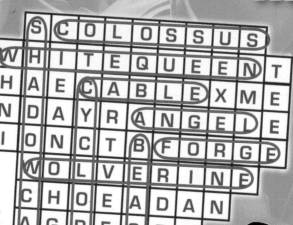

The X-Men are in the **DANGER ROOM**.

Sentinel **B** matches the original picture.

DESTINED FOR DANGER!

Path **C** is the correct route home to avoid the Sentinels.

ARMOUR ASSAULT!

COLOSSUS has the strength to overpower the Sentinel's armour.

COSMIC CONFUSION!

HEROES UNITED!

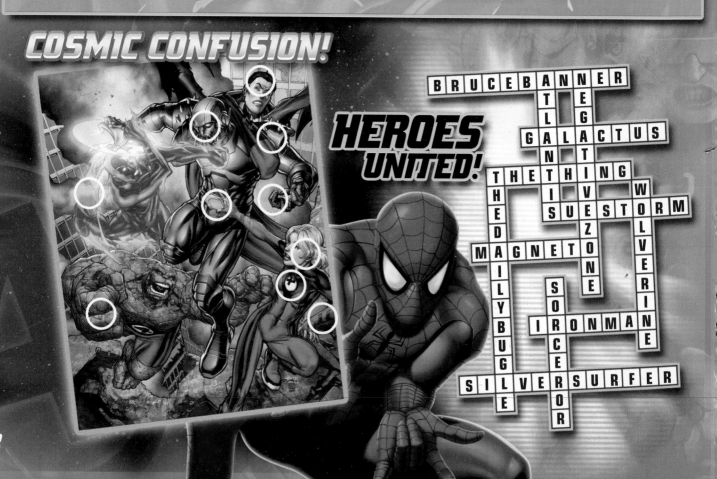

62